MW00778541

Published in 2023 by OH!
An Imprint of Welbeck Non-Fiction Limited,
part of Welbeck Publishing Group.
Based in London and Sydney.
www.welbeckpublishing.com

Disclaimer:
This book and the information contained herein are for general educational and entertainment use only. The contents are not claimed to be exhaustive, and the book is sold on the understanding that neither the publishers nor the author are thereby engaged in rendering any kind of professional services. Users are encouraged to confirm the information contained herein with other sources and review the information carefully with their appropriate, qualified service providers. Neither the publishers nor the author shall have any responsibility to any person or entity regarding any loss or damage whatsoever, direct or indirect, consequential, special or exemplary, caused or alleged to be caused, by the use or misuse of information contained in this book.

ISBN 978-1-80069-191-9

Editorial: Victoria Denne
Project manager: Russell Porter
Production: Jess Brisley

A CIP catalogue record for this book is available from the British Library

Printed in China

10 9 8 7 6 5 4 3 2 1

the little book of
AURAS

katalin patnaik

CONTENTS

CHAPTER

1

UNDERSTANDING the SEVEN AURIC LAYERS

Aura is the word we use for the electromagnetic radiation, the energy field, that everything is surrounded by.

Everything in this universe has an aura, whether it is a living being, or a lifeless object. People, animals, plants, rocks; even the book you are holding has an aura.

"A realized one sends out waves of spiritual influence in his aura, which draw many people towards him. Yet he may sit in a cave and maintain complete silence."

RAMANA MAHARISHI

Auras have been known to humanity since the dawn of time; they've been described in Hindu scriptures 6,000 years ago, and they are present in art from all around the world in the form of halos around the heads of spiritual and religious people and entities.

Throughout history, humans continued to research this mysterious energy field.

You might be surprised to hear, that scientists like Pythagoras, Avicenna, Paracelsus, Franz Anton Mesmer, Dr Walter Kilner, Alexander Gurwitsch, and even Nikola Tesla all researched auras in their fields of expertise.

The technology of aura photos that we all know is called Kirlian photography.

It is based on Tesla's experiments, and has been developed by scientists Semyon and Valentina Kirlian to show the colours of the aura on a polaroid photo.

Another technique that is becoming increasingly popular is called aura-imaging, developed by Guy Coggins, which is able to show our aura in real time on video.

Before you start to learn how to sense auras, ask yourself this question: why do I *want* to sense them?

What do I hope to gain from this ability? As the famous spiritual teacher Teal Swan says: "Us being able to see auras is nothing more than a party trick, unless it is a part of a deeper spiritual practice."

Being able to sense auras gives us the opportunity to help ourselves and others to heal and advance in our spiritual path, and to understand and connect with each other better.

the LAYERS of the AURA

The human aura has seven layers
that are connected to the seven
chakras, and that reflect different
aspects of the person they
belong to.

They all radiate from inside us, so
they overlap each other, reaching
further and further away from the
physical body.

the
SEVEN
LAYERS

the ETHERIC LAYER

The Etheric Layer is closest to our physical body, and it is the easiest to see for beginners.

This auric layer shows the status of our physical wellbeing and fitness.

It is connected to the root chakra, and has a steady greyish colour.

It extends up to a couple of inches from the physical body.

Poor physical health shows up as a dull Etheric Layer.

the EMOTIONAL LAYER

The emotional layer reflects our emotions, and just like our emotions, it changes in appearance throughout the day.

It is connected to the sacral chakra, and it could be any colour of the rainbow, depending on our current mood.

It can extend up to three inches from the physical body.

the MENTAL LAYER

The Mental Layer reflects our state of mind, our thoughts.

It is connected to the solar plexus chakra, and ideally has a bright yellow colour, strongest around the head.

It can extend up to eight inches from the physical body.

Poor mental health can show up as a dull Mental Layer.

the **ASTRAL**
LAYER

The Astral Layer reflects the status of our relationships with others.

It is connected to the heart chakra, and ideally it is a bright pink colour.

It can extend up to twelve inches from the physical body.

Poor interpersonal relationships and heartbreaks show up as a weak, dull Astral Layer.

the ETHERIC TEMPLATE LAYER

The Etheric Template Layer reflects us in this incarnation: our body, our identity, our personality and the energy we give off.

It is connected to the throat chakra, and can be any colour of the rainbow. It can extend up to two feet from the physical body.

This is the layer aura-healing therapists use to give complementary treatment to bodily ailments, and the one that shows up on aura photos.

the CELESTIAL LAYER

The Celestial Layer reflects our connection with the Divine, and the spirit world.

It is connected to the third eye chakra, and ideally is a bright white light surrounding us.

It can extend up to two and a half feet from the physical body.

An especially strong Celestial Layer indicates a highly spiritual person who may be able to communicate with the spirit world.

the CAUSAL LAYER

The Causal Layer, also called the Ketheric Template, reflects our soul and provides information about our soul's journey so far.

It is connected to the crown chakra, and ideally it is a bright white or golden colour.

It can extend to up to three feet from the physical body, and it "holds" all the other layers together, so it is especially bright.

An especially strong Causal Layer shows strong psychic abilities.

CHAPTER

2

PSYCHIC SENSING

Some people are born
with the ability to see
auras, but don't worry
if you're not one of
them! It can be learned.

There are different ways
to sense auras, so don't
lose heart if you can't
actually see them; you
might be someone who
feels, hears, or even
smells auras.

Think about which one
of your senses is the
strongest, and try to work
with that one.

Remember, sensing auras
is so much more than
seeing pretty colours.
All ways of sensing them
are equally valid.

LEARNING
to SEE
AURAS

PRACTICING on INANIMATE OBJECTS

You may find it easier to practice with inanimate objects first, because their auras don't change with time or their mood.

Pick an object with a solid colour, and stand it on a table in front of a white wall.

Focus on the object for a few seconds, then soften your focus, and shift your attention to your peripheral vision, on the wall behind the object.

Soon, you'll see the colour of your object surrounding it in the air.

When you are satisfied with your ability to see one object's aura, place another object with a solid colour behind it, but still visible to you, and do the exercise with both.

Build it up to 3–4 objects.

PRACTICING
on YOURSELF

Our eyes have evolved to focus on
things that are important for our
survival – that is, to focus on the
physical body of things that surround
us.

But we do have the ability to see
more than just that, using our
peripheral vision.

Start practicing with your hand against a white wall, or stand in front of a white wall with a mirror in your hands. Focus your eyes on your hand, or on your forehead in the mirror.

Now let your eyes relax without moving them, and shift your attention to your peripheral vision.

At first, you may see nothing, or just a kind of vibration in the air.

The more you practice, the more you'll be able to see.

At first, it might feel exhausting, but it will become easier with time, to the point of being able to see auras at all times.

"You attract damaged
people when you have
a healing spirit.
Be careful with that.
Because darkness is
drawn to your light."

SOVANJAN SARKAR

PRACTICING
on a FRIEND

Ask a friend to stand in front of a white wall. Focus your eyes on their forehead, and without moving your eyes, shift your attention to your peripheral vision.

When you see their aura surrounding them, ask them to gently sway from side to side.

Their aura should be dragged with them, making it easier for you to see. Don't be surprised if the colour of their aura changes as they move.

The colour of the aura depends on the layer you're looking at, potential strengths or problems within that area, and the person's mood.

tips and tricks

- You can blink during these exercises. The aura you saw may disappear for a fraction of a second, but don't worry, it will return.

- Some people find it easier to squint when looking at auras. If it doesn't happen with your eyes open but relaxed, try slightly squinting.

- When looking at other people's auras, let them know beforehand. You don't want them to feel alarmed because you're staring at them.

- Be gentle with your eyes! Do these exercises only for a few minutes at a time to avoid straining your eyes. Increase the duration of the exercises gradually.

LEARNING
to TOUCH
AURAS

Touching auras is like touching the wind, or the surface of still water.

It is an ethereal sensation we are not really used to, and it needs some practice to notice the slight change of energy when you touch a person's aura.

PRACTICING on INANIMATE OBJECTS

Everything has an aura, but some things are easier to sense than others. Crystals give off really strong vibrations, so it is a good idea to practice with one. Pick up your favourite crystal, ideally a palm stone, and close your eyes.

Pay attention to what you feel

- Does the crystal feel warm or cold?

- Does it make you feel happy, calm, or ready to conquer the world?

- Compare it to other stones.

- When you are confident with crystals, move on to other objects: plants, food, etc. are all good choices.

PRACTICING on YOUR OWN HAND

Hold your palms together in a prayer position. Rub them together gently until they feel warm.

Now gradually pull them apart, inch by inch, still making circular motions with them.

You will feel an energy field between them, at first maybe for an inch, but with practice at an increased distance.

You may even see the air move or shimmer between them.

PRACTICING
on OTHERS

Ask a friend to give their hand. Keep it in yours for a few moments, closing your eyes.

Listen to the impressions you have from holding their hand.

Now slowly make circular movements around it, gradually pulling yours further, feeling their aura.

Start practicing with hands, and gradually, when you feel more comfortable, move on to other body parts.

Eventually you will be able to feel the whole aura surrounding the body, and maybe even feel if there is anything out of order.

LEARNING
to SMELL
AURAS

It might sound strange, but you
can actually smell auras.

The smells you prefer refer to the current state of your aura. If, for example, you like the smell of the earth under your feet when walking in a forest, you are likely a well grounded person.

If you prefer flowery scents, you are likely to have a bubbly personality.

What someone smells like reflects on the state of their aura.

PRACTICING your SENSE of SMELL

Practice to recognize all kinds of smells. At home, try sniffing at spices, perfumes, food, dirty clothes; anything that has a smell.

When you are confident in your smell recognition, try smelling others – but don't be obnoxious about it.

- What do they smell like?

- Coffee and cigarettes?

- Overbearing cheap perfume?

- Mothballs and medicine?

Notice that just by reading these words, you have made mental images of people who are likely to smell like these examples.

Smelling auras works the exact same way: the smell a person emanates gives us information about their state of being.

LEARNING
to HEAR
AURAS

Hearing an aura doesn't mean you hear a buzzing sound following the person around, but rather making an image of the person's aura based on the quality and tone of their voice.

You can hear when someone is hesitant to speak, or when their words are dripping with sarcasm.

The way someone talks reflects on their health and their feelings, and so, on their aura.

At first you might find it easier to practice hearing auras when you are on the phone with someone, because there are no distractions: you can't see their clothing, facial expressions or hand gestures.

Pay attention to their voice

- Do they sound happy to talk to you, or would they rather be swimming in a pool of lava?

- Do they sound healthy, or do they clear their throat continuously?

- How does their voice make you feel, and why?

- Do they sound bossy, meek, sexy?

LEARNING
to SENSE
AURAS

Make a note of how you feel
around certain people.

- Do they make you feel at ease, or on guard?

- Does their presence fill the room, or do they hide in a corner to become invisible?

- What colour do they bring to mind?

- Are they the nerdy type, or are they the jock of the group?

Trust your gut! Don't let a person's physical appearance or their behaviour influence your intuition! They can lie, but their auras can't.

Make a note of your impressions in increasing detail, and follow them up after getting to know that person better.

"If your aura and energy become strong, then the unwanted slowly move away."

SHARMITA BHINDER

LEARNING
to see
AURAS in
MEDITATION

SHIELDING
and GROUNDING

Before doing any spiritual work, it is important to shield and ground yourself.

This is to protect you from negative energy during and after your work.

- Choose a time of the day when you don't have any distractions around you, ideally early morning, or just before you go to sleep.

- Get into a comfortable position sitting cross-legged, or laying down on the floor. Close your eyes and take slow, deep breaths.

- Concentrate on your body and let your muscles relax. With the intent of protecting yourself, imagine bright light surrounding you.

- Now imagine that a cord grows from you, deep within the earth, to anchor you. Send all your worries and pain that might trouble you through it, into the centre of the Earth, and ask for healing energy to fill their place.

You are now ready to do the meditation

MEDITATION

Imagine yourself in a place you feel comfortable in; your own room, a meadow with wild flowers, or just floating in space.

See yourself, and feel yourself, within your body. Now turn your attention to what surrounds your body. Put out your arms and feel the aura that surrounds you. What colour is it? How radiant, or dull, is it?

Spend some time exploring your aura. Pay attention to any details that come to you. Now slowly bring yourself back to the here and now.

Make notes of any details that came to you, and look up their meaning. Keeping a journal is a good idea to track how your aura changes with the time of the day and your mood.

When you feel confident in your meditation, start practicing on other people – asking for their consent first.

Ask a friend to sit with you, and to concentrate on a memory that brings up strong emotions. Ask them to write that memory and their emotion down on paper, but not to show you.

In your meditation, see your friend, and feel how they feel.

When you come out of your meditation, ask them whether you got it right.

CHAPTER
3

READING and INTERPRETING

the MEANING
of COLOURS
in the AURAS

As we have seen in the first chapter,
the aura consists of many layers.

When we talk about the colour of the aura, it is the overall colour, or colours, the person radiates at the moment.

The colour of a person's aura is not constant; it changes with our circumstances.

It is also influenced by our mood changes. Happiness, sadness or anger can change our colours – so can the intent to deceive and cheat, for example.

A person's aura is therefore indicative of their current state of mind and their intention towards us, too.

Try to sense the aura of an actor on stage or on screen, and compare it to their aura during an interview.

A good actor will have the aura of the character surrounding them while acting, and change back to their own colours when they are not performing.

A brilliant aura shows the positive side
of the interpretation of its colour, while
a dull aura shows a reversed, blocked
meaning.

the PRIMARY COLOURS

There are seven primary colours of the aura, which are connected to individual chakras. Different shades of these colours boil down to the same basic meaning given here, but provide nuances to it.

RED

is the colour
associated with the
root chakra.

If a person's aura is mainly red,
they are a passionate and sensual
person, who loves to enjoy life.

They are very active and don't
spend time procrastinating; they'll
jump into action as soon as they
have an idea.

They know what they want, and
they are well grounded
in reality.

A dull red aura shows a person who is blocked from this type of lifestyle.

They may be experiencing burnout, holding a grudge, or grieving for something or someone, and it stops them from enjoying life.

In other senses, a red aura is:

Touch: warm or hot

Sound: sexy

Smell: sweet and pleasant

Intuition: sensual

ORANGE

is the colour
associated with the
sacral chakra.

If a person's aura is mainly orange, they are a happy-go-lucky person who loves other people's company.

They are outgoing, friendly, and always ready to be there for others.

They love trying out new things, they are very creative, and are good at teamwork.

A dull orange aura shows a person who experiences the flip side of this.

They may be obsessive, jealous, while at the same time they may have problems with commitment.

They may also have trouble with addictions.

In other senses, an orange aura is:

Touch: spiky

Sound: lively

Smell: spicy

Intuition: impulsive, spontaneous

YELLOW

is the colour
associated with the
solar plexus chakra.

If a person's aura is mainly yellow, they are intelligent, confident, ambitious, and have a healthy self-esteem.

They are inspiring personalities, and often find themselves as role models for others.

They have a positive thing to say to everyone, and can make the situation look less difficult just with their presence.

A dull yellow aura shows a person who may use their heads without their hearts.

Someone who is overly critical, an uncompromising perfectionist towards themselves and others.

In other senses, a yellow aura is:

Touch: prickly

Sound: melodious

Smell: citrusy

Intuition: energetic

GREEN

is the colour associated with the heart chakra.

If a person's aura is mainly green,
they are loving and caring towards
others, or they might be in love
with someone.

They are natural healers, even if they
are not in the medical profession.

They do whatever they can to help
others feel better. They are also
assertive and well balanced.

A dull green aura shows a bitter
person who is jealous, envious of
others, and who doesn't take
criticism well.

In other senses, a green aura is:

Touch: uneven

Sound: deep

Smell: fresh

Intuition: healthy, confident

BLUE

is the colour
associated with the
throat chakra.

If a person's aura is mainly blue, they are great communicators, and are truthful and honest.

They value honesty and loyalty in their partners, and they are always there to defend their loved ones and what they believe is right.

They are dependable and clear a bout their intentions.

A dull blue aura shows a person who is less than trustworthy, and who can be easily swayed in their beliefs.

They find it hard to talk about their feelings.

In other senses, a blue aura is:

Touch: cold

Sound: smooth

Smell: smoky

Intuition: thoughtful

INDIGO

is the colour associated with the Third Eye chakra.

If a person's aura is mainly indigo, they are very intuitive and sensitive to their surroundings.

They might often have a déjà vu feeling, or have other psychic abilities, like clairvoyance or prophetic dreams.

They are born seekers, and they enjoy being part of a religion, once they find where they feel they belong.

A dull indigo aura shows a person who may be going through the so-called "dark night of the soul", with doubts and fears of being in the wrong place.

In other senses, an indigo aura is:

Touch: smooth

Sound: clear and pleasant

Smell: lavender and
similar herbs

Intuition: magical, witchy

PURPLE

is the colour associated with the crown chakra.

If a person's aura is mainly purple, they are charismatic leaders who are on a mission to make this world a better place.

They have a close connection with the spirit world and the Universe, and are highly empathetic.

They don't concern themselves with materialistic trivialities.

They love learning and sharing their knowledge.

A dull purple aura shows someone with a false sense of grandiosity.

They are prone to psychological disorders.

In other senses, a purple aura is:

Touch: pulsating

Sound: murmuring

Smell: soothing and mild

Intuition: spiritual

WHITE

A pure white aura is extremely rare. Maybe only a handful of human souls on Earth have one.

It is more common to see white patches in someone's aura.

This means they are very spiritually inclined, or that they are aligned with their higher purpose in this incarnation.

White patches around certain body parts also mean that those parts are used excessively at the moment. For example, an author in the process of writing their next book would have white around their head.

"The energy of our thoughts, words, actions and emotions collectively creates the frequency of our vibrational aura."

ALARIC HUTCHINSON

SECONDARY COLOURS

Secondary colours, or colours that are shades of the primary ones, are closely related in meaning to their nearest primary colour, with an added layer of nuance. Below are the most common secondary colours.

LAVENDER

A person with a lavender aura has little to no care for the mundane.

They love everything magical and spiritual, and are happiest when they are left alone with their inner world.

It shows the phase of healing, and inner work.

A dull lavender aura might indicate
a person who is prone to be lost in
their imagination, and can't see
reality as it is.

They might distance themselves from
others, and turn completely inward.

In other senses, a lavender aura is:

Touch: smooth and even

Sound: twinkling

Smell: lavender

Intuition: otherworldly

AQUAMARINE

combines the blues and the greens of the spectrum; they are imaginative and magical, but also know how to keep their feet on the ground.

They are compassionate and helpful,
and like to see people succeed.

They are often teachers or healers,
or have a healing effect on others.

They generally have good health,
both mental and physical.

A dull aquamarine aura can mean that the person has gone to the extremes of one aspect of their personality, for example they have concentrated too long on standing with both feet on the ground, and haven't been in touch with their spirituality.

They need to balance their mundane and spiritual lives.

In other senses, an aquamarine
aura is:

Touch: unpolished but smooth

Sound: enticing

Smell: ocean breeze, fresh

Intuition: intelligent and
refined

TURQUOISE

A person with a
turquoise aura has
a healthy view of
their strengths and
weaknesses.

They aren't deluding themselves, and they are ready to provide constructive criticism to others as well, while remaining helpful and kind.

They radiate a sense of confidence and peace with themselves that inspires others, too.

A dull turquoise aura may indicate that the person is going through a phase when they need to concentrate on themselves, and have little time or energy to give to others – like around end-of-year exams, or a promotion.

In other senses, a turquoise aura is:

Touch: polished and smooth

Sound: like twirling water

Smell: tasty

Intuition: influential

PINK

A person with a
pink aura is loving
and kind.

They welcome everyone with an open heart, and they can be counted on when one needs a shoulder to cry on.

People who have recently fallen in love, or who feel very passionate about someone – like their children, their friends, their parents – also have pink in their aura.

A dull pink aura indicates irresponsibility and fickleness.

The person is not ready to commit to anything at the moment, and only wants to have fun.

In other senses, a pink aura is:

Touch: soft, light

Sound: quiet, soft-spoken

Smell: cotton candy

Intuition: cute, endearing

SILVER

is quite rare to see,
but it is possible.

A silver aura indicates fertility, and the early phases of creation – not only in pregnancy. It shows self-confidence and being attuned to one's higher self.

A person with a silver aura can often be caught daydreaming, and can be a bit moody.

A dull silver aura shows someone who finds it hard to be themselves around others, and has difficulty at being assertive.

In other senses, a silver aura is:

Touch: metallic

Sound: clear and melodious

Smell: vanilla

Intuition: creative, motherly

PATTERNS
and other
SIGNS

"We all have auras. But it is much easier to see the aura of someone who is in a state of samadhi or other profound state of awareness."

FREDERICK LENZ

Streaks or channels of light

mean a person is receiving energy from a source that is outside of their aura. This could be thoughts and prayers from their well-wishers, or support from the spirit realm.

Orbs

appear when a person's spirit guide is around them, hovering just above their shoulder.

Patches of colours

above chakras hint at the energy level of those chakras.

A bright yellow patch around the head means the person often uses their mind to solve problems – like a student, or a writer, while a bright yellow patch above the root chakra may mean pregnancy, or the person's desire to have children.

A hole

in the aura means an injury or
disease in the body part it is around.

A dent

in the aura suggests the need for the
person to shield, as they easily give
away their energy.

If the energy flow in an aura is not
continuous and steady, there may be a
problem starting at that area of the body.
Chaotic swirls, a jagged or frozen flow of
energy all hint at troubles with health.

Remember:

Never give a medical diagnosis based on your findings.

If you suspect health problems, without alarming the person you're reading for, gently advise them to see a doctor for a check-up.

CHAPTER

4

SEALING and PROTECTING

As we go through our
day, we encounter a
multitude of energies, not
all of which are benevolent.

An angry boss, a traffic
jam, a jealous friend;
there are people and
entities all around us who
can drain our energy
and damage our aura.

In addition to not letting them take your power from you by giving them importance, here are a few rituals and exercises you can do to protect yourself.

- Trust your abilities.

- Everyone is capable of magic.

- The secret to success is in your intent.

To protect yourself spiritually in general, perform the grounding and shielding exercises in Chapter 2.

SMOKE
and
SMUDGING

Clearing away negative energies
with smoke is a worldwide
practice.

Make sure you have a window open nearby, especially if you are using chillies, as they are extremely powerful.

Nowadays smudging with sage is very popular, but using bay leaves, dry red chillies or rosemary works just as well, and might be culturally more appropriate, and also more sustainable.

Be aware that some of the sage available on the market has been harvested by poachers, so try to research your seller before you buy.

With the intention of clearing away any negative energy, light your herbs, and wave them around yourself to surround yourself with smoke.

Concentrate on your intent, and see with your mind's eye as all the negative energy clears away, and is replaced with love and light.

CUTTING the CORD

When we are influenced by others, a cord forms between our auras. When we are angry or resentful towards someone, or hurt by what they have done, that cord takes away our energy.

To stop this from happening, imagine a cord starting from your belly button. It connects you to the person or thing that has hurt you.

Concentrate on the intention of severing yourself from their influence. Imagine holding the cord with one hand, and cut it with an imaginary scissor.

Acknowledge that the bond is now broken, and you are no longer under their influence.

CHAPTER

5

HEALING
your AURAS

Because our auric layers are the subtle manifestations of our physical, mental and spiritual wellbeing, they can be healed and balanced in a multitude of ways.

Remember:

The exercises
and rituals in this
chapter are only meant
to be complementary
therapies to your
ongoing treatment
and conscious steps
towards your goal.

These exercises will help you balance or strengthen your aura, and attract changes and new opportunities into your life.

At the end of this chapter, you will find a summary of correspondences for each auric layer that you can use with the techniques below.

Remember:

Consult your doctor
before making any
changes in your
lifestyle, especially if
you have an ongoing
health condition or if
you are pregnant.

CREATING an ALTER

An altar doesn't necessarily have to be a religious space. You may view it as a vision board, if you like.

An altar doesn't have to be extravagant, either. If you don't have much space in your home, it can even be arranged in a corner of your bedside table. You can use any items you like. Be creative!

What matters is that you see the altar every day, so it can inspire you to work towards your goals.

COLOUR THERAPY

Wear the colour of the auric layer you want to strengthen!

You will have noticed that red clothes make people look sexy and confident, while blue ones make them look sophisticated and level-headed.

Include your colours in your appearance, even if it is only in the form of a tie or an earring. Build their presence up gradually, if you are not confident at first.

You can also bring these colours into the interior of your home.

CRYSTAL TREATMENT

Each crystal has a specific spiritual quality. Using them near their corresponding chakras is like a day at the spa for that energy centre, that re-energizes your aura. Research which crystal you need for a specific task.

Perform your shielding and grounding exercise, laying down on the floor. Imagine the chakra and the auric layer you want to heal.

Place the corresponding crystals above the chakra on your body, and enjoy their vitalizing effect.

Stay like this for a few minutes, until you feel the crystal has refilled your energy, then come out of meditation, and cleanse the crystal.

YOGA ASANAS

Each auric layer is connected to a chakra, and each chakra has specific yoga exercises to balance them.

It is important to do these exercises properly, as some of them may cause injuries. Consult a yoga instructor to discuss the more demanding asanas, and to ask whether you should be doing them.

MINDFULNESS

Being mindful of our actions is a great way to strengthen our aura. Start a journal, and at the end of each day, answer the questions given in the list of correspondences.

As time goes by and this becomes a habit, you will become increasingly in control of your actions.

Taking responsibility is hugely empowering, and leads to a radiant aura.

AFFIRMATIONS

Affirmations are a form of positive self-talk, and they help us to get into the right mindset to achieve our goals.

Repeat them
when you
feel your will
faltering,
with intention
and faith in
their power.

list of
correspondences
for the

AURIC
LAYERS

As we have seen in Chapter 3, everything is interconnected. We can influence the energy we radiate by using tools corresponding with our goals.

The following pages provide corresponding tools for each auric layer. Use these to strengthen or balance out specific layers, and reaffirm your intention. Remember: using these tools will ease your way to your goals, but won't replace the work you need to put into achieving them!

the ETHERIC LAYER

Reflects: our physical wellbeing and fitness

Helps: physical wellbeing, grounding, stability, safety, wealth

Chakra: root chakra

Colour: red

Body part: bones

Glands: testicles and ovaries

Crystals: agate, tiger's eye, onyx, smoke quartz

Asanas: setu bandhasana, vajrasana, utkatasana

Incense: cedarwood, myrrh, pachouli

Questions:

- Have I respected my body/money today?

- How did I take care of it?

- What could be even better?

Affirmations:

- I am accountable for myself.
- I take care of my body/money.
- I love my body.
- I allow myself to be money-minded.

the EMOTIONAL LAYER

Reflects: our emotions

Helps: joy, creativity, letting go

Chakra: sacral chakra

Colour: orange

Body part: reproductive organs, bladder, circulatory system

Glands: adrenal

Crystals: citrine, carnelian, golden topaz

Asanas: utkata konasana, mandukasana, supta baddha konasana

Incense: jasmine, rose, sandalwood

Questions:

- Am I open to changes and opportunities?

- How have I expressed my needs today?

Affirmations:

- I am enough.
- I deserve to enjoy life.
- I have the right to express myself.

the MENTAL LAYER

Reflects: our state of mind

Helps: focus, purposefulness, self-confidence, endurance, abundance

Chakra: solar plexus chakra

Colour: yellow

Body part: digestive system, muscles

Glands: pancreas

Crystals: yellow citrine, aventurine, sunstone

Asanas: bhujangasana, dhanurasana, parivrtta trikonasana

Incense: vetiver, bergamot, cinnamon

Questions:

- Have I taken the lead today?

- Was I confident in all situations?

- How could I improve how people treat me?

Affirmations:

- I bring out the best in myself.

- I respect my boundaries.

- I choose what I spend my energy on.

the ASTRAL LAYER

Reflects: our relationship with others

Helps: balance, acceptance, forgiveness, love and romance

Chakra: heart chakra

Colour: pink and green

Body part: heart, chest, lungs, circulatory system

Glands: thymus

Crystals: rose quartz, malachite, moonstone, jade

Asanas: anuvittasana, ustrasana, ardha matsyendrasana

Incense: rose, bergamot, honey grass

Questions:

- How judgemental am I with myself and with others?

- Have I followed my heart today?

Affirmations:

- I love myself and my potentials.

- I give love and sympathy to everyone, including myself.

the ETHERIC TEMPLATE LAYER

Reflects: our self in this incarnation

Helps: self-awareness, creativity, communication

Chakra: throat chakra

Colour: blue

Body part: neck, ears, mouth

Glands: thyroid

Crystals: turquoise, lapis lazuli, aquamarine, sapphire

Asanas: sarvangasana, halasana, simhasana

Incense: chamomile, myrrh

Questions:

- How have I expressed myself today?

- What could I have said clearer?

- How did I use my creativity today?

Affirmations:

- I talk about my feelings and needs clearly, without resentment.

- What I say is worthy of people's attention.

the CAUSAL LAYER

Reflects: our soul's journey so far

Helps: connection to the divine

Chakra: crown chakra

Colour: violet, gold, white

Body part: the upper part of the skull, cerebral cortex, skin

Glands: pineal gland

Crystals: clear quartz, amethyst, diamond, milk quartz

Asanas: sirsasana, shavasana

Incense: lavender, frankincense, rose tree

Questions:

- Have I displayed any inherited, impulsive behaviour?

- Did I listen to my higher self when making decisions?

- Have I made space for the divine in my life?

Affirmations:

- I am more than just my body and the roles I play.

- I am proud that I want my life to be more than meaningless mundanity.

"Be consistent in maintaining an aura of grace and love."

MEGGAN ROXANNE